To my beloved Nigel,
Thank you for teaching me to Roar!

Design, Edited and Illustrated: © Mary Adetayo
First Printing, 2023
ISBN 9798852606631

In the heart of the African plains,
where the sun's golden rays illuminate the land,
Lies a majestic savannah,
where nature's creatures harmoniously stand.

Meet Leo, a lion with a mighty roar,
his presence bold and grand,
Known throughout the vast expanse
for the strength of his command.
But amidst the wild beauty,
another soul dwells, fierce and free,
Leona, a lioness with an independent spirit,
hunting with agility.

She roams the grassy plains,
her eyes filled with an untamed fire,
Yet unaware of the power that lies within her,
waiting to inspire.

Through golden grasslands, a fleet-footed antelope bounds,
Leo and Leona give chase, with passion resound.
The thunder of their paws, the symphony of the hunt,
Their paths cross, an electric moment, a rhythmic front.

Leo, captivated by Leona's strength and allure,
His eyes shimmer with admiration, hearts both pure.
They pause in the chase, a conversation ignites,
In the rhythm of their words, their connection takes flight.

Together they venture,
on a rhythmic journey they embark,
Through golden grasslands,
under the vast sky's sparkling arc.
Leona listens intently,
as Leo shares the secrets of his might,
Teaching her the rhythms of the wild,
under the moon's gentle light.

Leona reveals a secret, a truth yet unspoken,
She has never roared, her voice yet unbroken.
Leo's spirit stirs, a desire to guide and inspire,
He vows to help her find her voice, to set her soul afire.

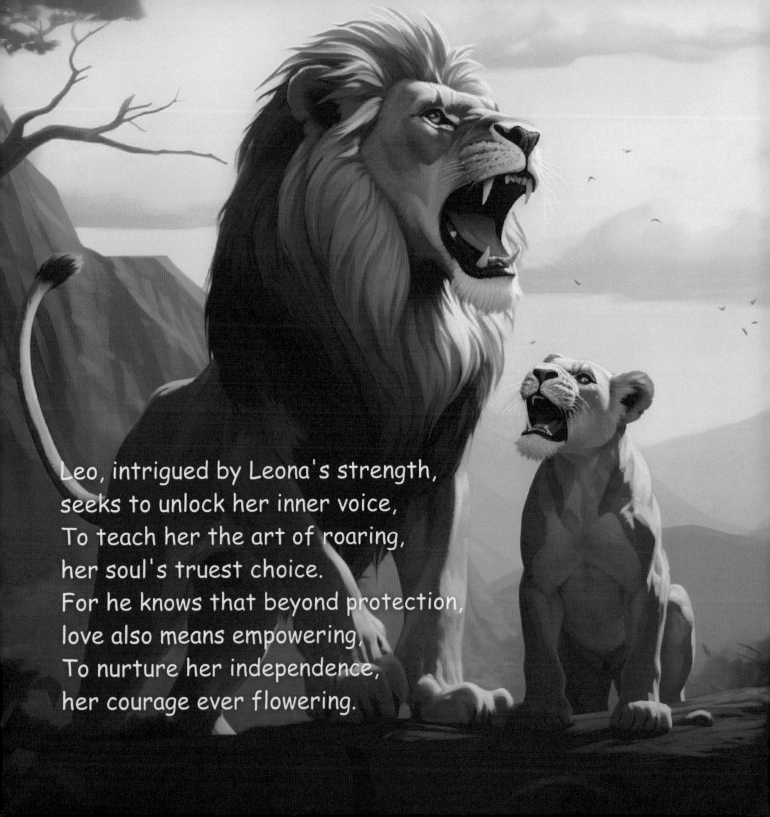

Leo, intrigued by Leona's strength,
seeks to unlock her inner voice,
To teach her the art of roaring,
her soul's truest choice.
For he knows that beyond protection,
love also means empowering,
To nurture her independence,
her courage ever flowering.

Under the golden African sun,
Leo and Leona embark on a rhythmic quest,
A chapter of roaring lessons,
where their spirits are put to the test.
Leo, with wisdom and grace,
takes Leona under his wing,
To teach her the art of roaring,
a gift that only lions can bring.

In a thunderous roar, Leo shares tales of
protection and might,
A signal to claim their territory, a symphony that ignites.
With a soft rumble, he whispers of love, a gentle melody,
A roar that soothes and comforts,
connecting souls so free.

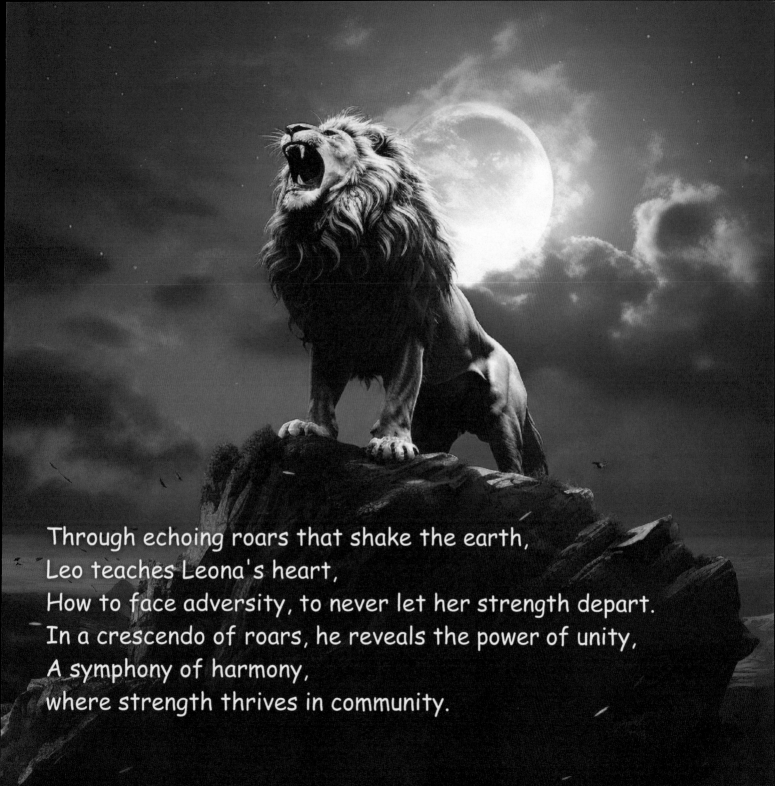

Through echoing roars that shake the earth,
Leo teaches Leona's heart,
How to face adversity, to never let her strength depart.
In a crescendo of roars, he reveals the power of unity,
A symphony of harmony,
where strength thrives in community.

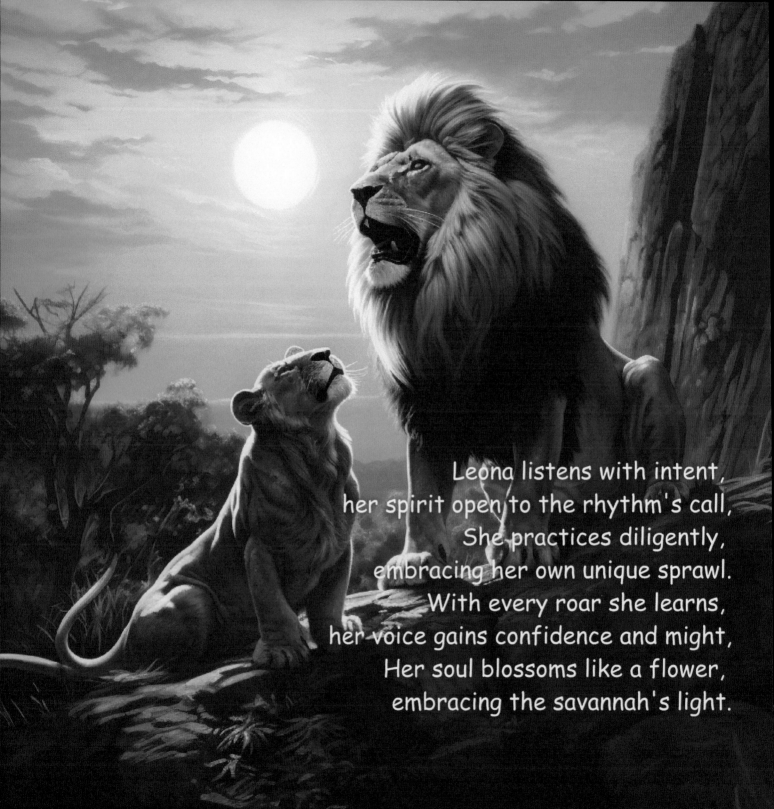

Leona listens with intent,
her spirit open to the rhythm's call,
She practices diligently,
embracing her own unique sprawl.
With every roar she learns,
her voice gains confidence and might,
Her soul blossoms like a flower,
embracing the savannah's light.

In the stillness of the night,
under a starlit sky so vast,
Leona finds her own voice,
her roar powerful and steadfast.
With Leo's guidance and unwavering support,
she finds her place,
A lioness roaring with conviction,
an embodiment of grace.

With each passing day,
Leona's roars grow strong,
Her soul, like the savannah,
sings a captivating song.
Leo, the lion of wisdom,
knows her strength will rise,
He urges her to trust in herself,
to see through her own eyes.

In the face of danger, they navigate with grace,
Leona's independence guiding them in every chase.
Through dense forests and rivers that fiercely flow,
Her confidence surges, a rhythm that begins to glow.

Leo, the guardian, watches with pride in his eyes,
As Leona roars with strength, her soul ready to rise.
He reassures her, that though they journey side by side,
Her independence is vital, her strength a rhythmic stride.

In the heart of the wild,
danger lurks in the shadows deep,
A rogue lion emerges, threatening their pride's keep.
Leo and Leona stand tall, their courage set aflame,
In this chapter of bravery, they shall rise to reclaim.

Their territory, once serene, now faces turmoil and strife,
Leo and Leona face the challenge, their rhythm alive.
Leo, with his mighty presence,
commands attention and respect,
Leona, fierce and agile, her spirit steadfastly elects.

Together, they devise a plan, a symphony of strategy,
To protect their pride, showcasing their newfound bravery.
Drawing upon their newfound skills and unity profound,
They combine their roars, a force that shall astound.

In the test of courage, their teamwork takes flight,
Leo and Leona, a rhythm of strength, shining bright.
They flank the rogue, a seamless choreography,
Their roars and cunningness, a symphony of victory.

As the battle unfolds, their prowess comes to light,
Leona's agility, a dance of courage taking flight.
Leo's mighty roars, a powerful anthem of defence,
Together, their unity prevails, a testament immense.

Through the rhythm of their cooperation,
their pride stands strong,
A force that can conquer any foe, where they belong.
Their unity inspires the pride, filling the air with awe,
For Leo and Leona's bravery, a rhythm without flaw.

With the rogue lion defeated, peace returns to their domain,
Leo and Leona, triumphant, their strength forever reigns.
In the symphony of their courage,
they've proven their worth,
A chapter of bravery, a tale of their rhythmic birth.

Hailed as heroes by their pride, they stand tall,
Their exceptional qualities, admired by all.
Leo, the king, and Leona, the queen,
Their reign begins, their rhythm serene.

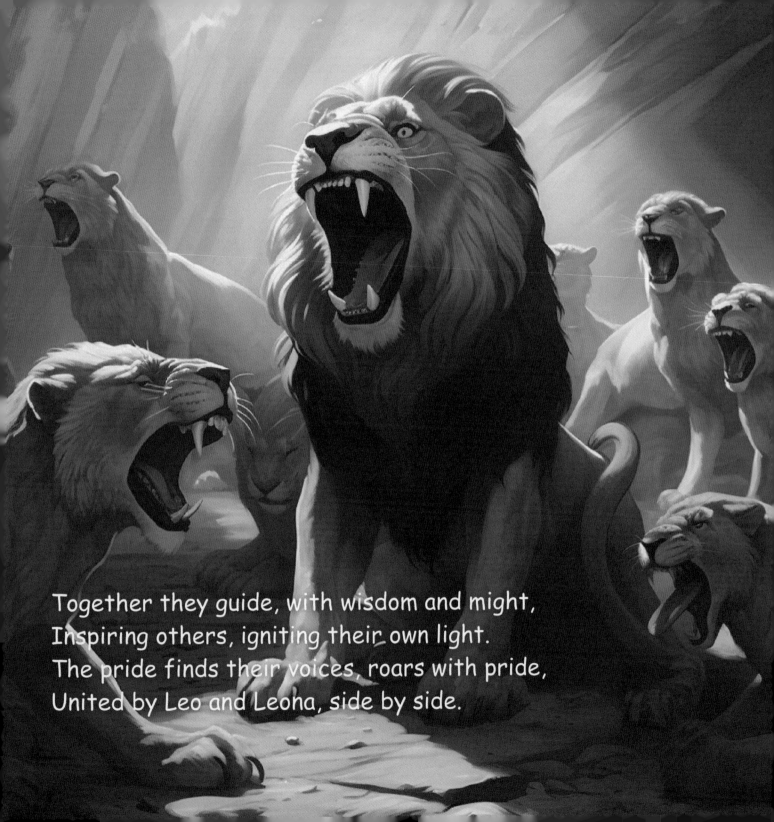

Together they guide, with wisdom and might,
Inspiring others, igniting their own light.
The pride finds their voices, roars with pride,
United by Leo and Leona, side by side.

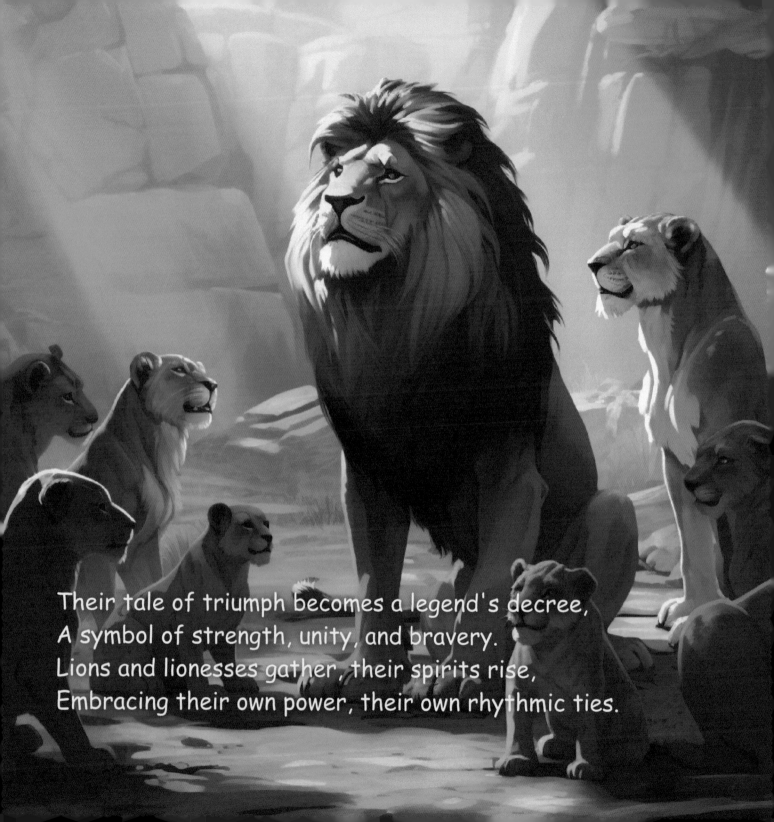

Their tale of triumph becomes a legend's decree,
A symbol of strength, unity, and bravery.
Lions and lionesses gather, their spirits rise,
Embracing their own power, their own rhythmic ties.

As the sun sets on the horizon, casting its golden glow,
Leo and Leona stand together, leaders of the pride below.
Renowned and revered, their spirits shine so bright,
Guiding their pride through day and night.

The rhythm of their guidance echoes through the years,
Each cub finding their voice, releasing their fears.
Leo and Leona, their legacy forever engrained,
In the hearts of the pride, their wisdom sustained.

And as the final pages turn, the story finds its close,
A rhythmic journey through love, strength, and prose.
The epilogue leaves us with a lingering thought,
To find our own rhythms, the battles we've fought.

And so, the book concludes with a rhythmic sigh,
Leo and Leona's love soaring, forever in the sky.
The final message lingers, like a whisper in the wind,
Embrace your rhythm, find your roar,
let your true self begin.

Printed in Great Britain
by Amazon

31715283R00021